PROBE POWER

HOW SPACE PROBES DO WHAT HUMANS CAN'T

AILYNN COLLINS

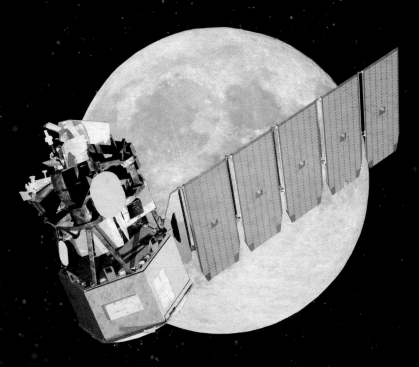

CONTENT CONSULTANT
SARAH RUIZ
Aerospace Engineer

CAPSTONE PRESS
a capstone imprint

Edge Books are published by Capstone Press.
1710 Roe Crest Drive, North Mankato, Minnesota 56003
www.capstonepub.com

Library of Congress Cataloging-in-Publication Data
Names: Collins, Ailynn, 1964– author.
Title: Probe power : how space probes do what humans can't / by Ailynn Collins.
Description: North Mankato, Minnesota : Capstone Press, [2019] | Series: Edge books.
Future space | "Edge Books is published by Capstone Press." | Audience: Ages 8–9. |
Audience: K to grade 3. Identifiers: LCCN 2019004851
ISBN 9781543572773 (ebook pdf) | ISBN 9781543572698 (hardcover)
ISBN 9781543575187 (pbk.)
Subjects: LCSH: Space probes—Juvenile literature. | Extrasolar planets—Juvenile literature.
| Outer space—Exploration—Juvenile literature. Classification: LCC TL795.3 .C65 2019 | DDC
629.43/5—dc23
LC record available at https://lccn.loc.gov/2019004851

Editorial Credits
Michelle Parkin, editor; Laura Mitchell, designer; Jo Miller, media researcher;
Katy LaVigne, production specialist

Photo Credits
NASA, Cover (Probe), 1 (Probe), 7, 15, 16, Goddard's Conceptual Image Lab/B. Monroe, 28, Johns
Hopkins APL/Steve Gribben, 19, JPL/Cornell University, 25; Newscom: Cover Images/JAXA etc.,
22, EyePress EPN/ISRO, 17, Photoshot/Bettina Strenske, 21; Shutterstock: Belish, Cover (Moon), 1
(Moon), Cristi Matel, 9, David Herraez Calzada, 12-13, WeAre, 5; Wikimedia: NASA/JHU APL/SwRI/
Steve Gribben, 11, NASA/JPL, 27

Design Elements
Capstone; Shutterstock: Audrius Birbilas

TABLE OF CONTENTS

CHAPTER ONE

THE MYSTERY OF SPACE

Humans have been curious about space since we first looked up at the night sky. Astronauts have rocketed off Earth and explored outer space. They've stepped foot on the moon. They've even lived in space at the **International Space Station** (ISS).

Currently, humans can only travel so far. Still, this hasn't stopped scientists from wondering what else is out in the far reaches of space. But how do we discover the mysteries of space if they are too far for humans to get to? We use space probes!

International Space Station—a place for astronauts to live and work in space

CHAPTER TWO

SEND IN THE PROBES

A space probe is a robotic spacecraft. Rockets launch the probe into space. There are no astronauts onboard. The probe is controlled by high-tech computers. It carries special equipment to collect information about what it discovers. Scientists and **engineers** on Earth watch the probe's journey.

A space probe can be as large as a school bus or as tiny as a cracker, depending on its mission. Some probes land on moons or planets. Others take pictures of space objects.

SPACE FACT:

The world's smallest space probe is called Sprite. It is the size of a Saltine cracker. It is 400 miles (644 kilometers) above us, orbiting Earth.

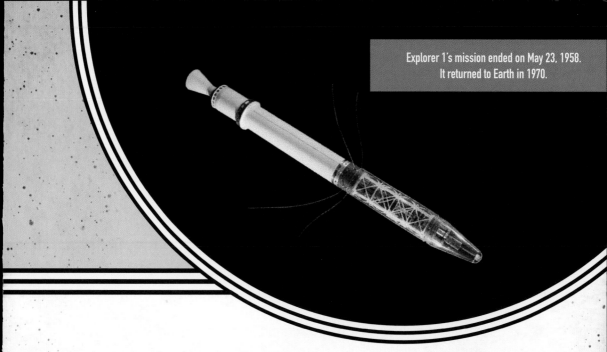

Countries all around the world have sent probes into space, including the United States, Russia, China, France, and India. The first space probe sent into **orbit** was Sputnik 1. The Soviet Union, which later became Russia, launched Sputnik 1 in 1957. A few months later, NASA sent the probe Explorer 1 into orbit. All of these early probes studied Earth from space.

SPACE FACT:

NASA stands for the National Aeronautics and Space Administration. Its headquarters is in Washington, D.C.

engineer—someone trained to design and build machines, vehicles, bridges, roads, and other structures

orbit—the path an object follows as it goes around the sun or a planet

A PROBE'S JOB

As technology advanced, scientists sent probes farther into space to study other planets, moons, and **asteroids**.

Today there are three kinds of space probes—interplanetary probes, orbiters, and landers. Some probes have powerful telescopes to study far-away stars and planets. Some fly around in space, while others orbit one object. Still others land on planets and conduct experiments.

Space probes must be able to withstand extreme environments and function properly for long periods of time. Not all probes are successful. Some crash into the object they're supposed to land on. Some simply don't work. But scientists learn from these mistakes. They continue to make better spacecraft for the future.

asteroid—a chunk of rock that orbits the sun; asteroids are too small to be called planets

An orbiter probe travels around Earth.

CHAPTER THREE

INTERPLANETARY PROBES

Interplanetary probes fly past objects in space. These objects can be planets, moons, stars, asteroids, or objects we haven't discovered yet. As it flies by, the probe captures images. It also gathers information about the material the object is made of, as well as the object's shape, size, and **atmosphere**.

One of the most exciting interplanetary probes in space today is New Horizons. The probe flew past the **dwarf planet** Pluto in 2015. New Horizons was the first probe to study Pluto up close. After this mission ended, the probe went on to study objects in the Kuiper Belt. This area is beyond Neptune. It contains space rocks and other icy objects.

atmosphere—the layer of gases that surrounds some planets, dwarf planets, and moons

dwarf planet—a space sphere that orbits the sun but has not cleared the orbit of neighboring planets

The New Horizons probe collected information from Pluto.

Scientists want to know what kind of material is in the Kuiper Belt. They've made educated guesses but they don't know for sure. Scientists also want to study the rocks that float nearby. One of those space rocks is called Ultima Thule.

SPACE FACT:

Ultima Thule is 1 billion miles (1.6 billion km) past Pluto.

The Madrid Deep Space communication complex is part of NASA's Deep Space Network.

On January 1, 2019, New Horizons made contact with Earth, confirming it had flown by Ultima Thule. This is the farthest that any probe has traveled to explore a planetary body. When New Horizons sent images back to Earth, scientists saw the first pictures of this far-away space rock.

SPACE FACT:

New Horizons's radio message was picked up by NASA's Deep Space Network antenna in Madrid, Spain.

CHAPTER FOUR

ORBITERS

Orbiter probes are designed to collect data from a certain planet or moon. Orbiters travel around their object, take pictures, and send the information back to scientists on Earth.

The Hubble Space Telescope is an orbiter. It is the size of a school bus and weighs as much as two elephants. The Hubble has been orbiting Earth for almost 30 years, taking pictures of distant stars and objects in deep space. Soon its mission will end.

A new space telescope will begin its mission in 2021. The James Webb Space Telescope will orbit the sun. It is bigger than the Hubble and will help scientists see even more of the universe. The James Webb will study **black holes**. Hopefully it will send back pictures of objects that we've never seen before.

Other orbiters have been studying planets in our **solar system**. NASA, together with two European space agencies, launched the Cassini probe in 1997. Cassini began to orbit the planet Saturn in 2004. It was the biggest and most expensive probe ever launched.

Cassini studied Saturn and its icy moons for more than 10 years. It traveled 4.9 billion miles (7.9 billion km) and orbited Saturn 294 times.

black hole—an area of space with such a strong gravitational field that not even light can escape it

solar system—the sun and all the planets, moons, comets, and smaller bodies orbiting it

The Japanese probe Akatsuki began orbiting the planet Venus in 2015. Earth and Venus are often called twin planets. They are about the same size. They were also formed around the same time. But the planets are very different. The surface of Venus is too hot for humans to survive. Earth's atmosphere has oxygen, which humans need to live. Akatsuki is studying Venus' atmosphere, which is mostly carbon dioxide. It also has clouds made of sulfuric acid, a dangerous chemical for humans.

The Akatsuki probe studied the thick clouds that cover Venus.

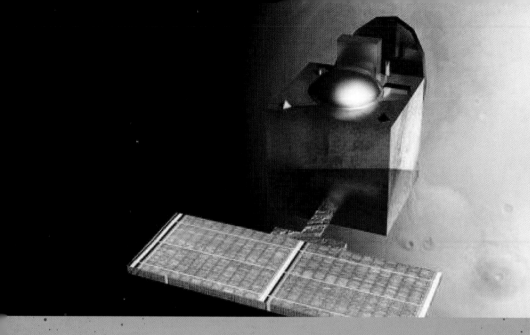

The Mangalyaan probe has been orbiting Mars since September 24, 2014.

In 2013 India became the fourth country to successfully send a probe to Mars. Its probe is called Mars Orbiter Mission, or Mangalyaan. Using this probe, scientists are studying Mars's atmosphere and surface. India hopes to have more missions to Mars. One day it may send astronauts to explore the planet.

SPACE FACT:

Mangalyaan means "Mars craft" in Sanskrit. Sanskrit is an ancient Indian language.

Scientists study the sun and how it affects planets. Earth is 93 million miles (149 million km) away from the sun. Getting closer to the sun's surface will help scientists learn more about it. On November 4, 2018, the Parker Solar Probe got closer to the sun than any other human-made object before it. By 2024 the probe will be even closer—3.83 million miles (6.2 million km) away.

To stay in one piece, Parker has to withstand incredible heat—about 2,500 degrees Fahrenheit (1,371 degrees Celsius). That's about 25 times hotter than a hot summer day on Earth!

The Parker Solar Probe was built with a shield to protect it from the sun's heat. It also has a cooling system to keep its equipment safe. Scientists believe this probe will show them what happens on the sun's surface and how **solar flares** affect Earth.

solar flare—gas that shoots out of the sun's surface

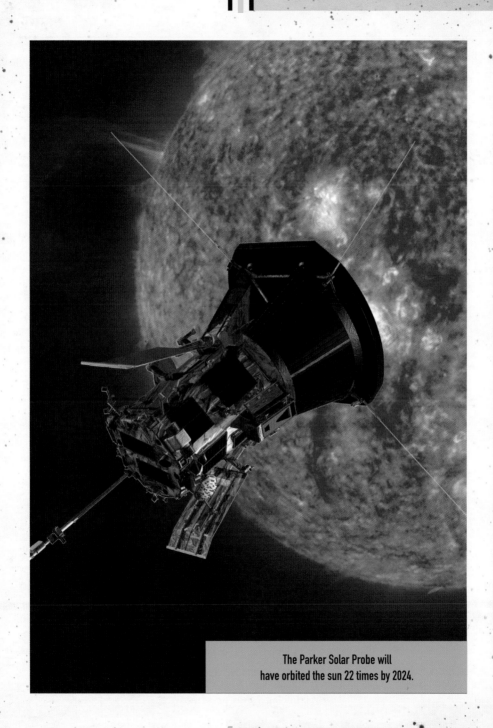

The Parker Solar Probe will have orbited the sun 22 times by 2024.

CHAPTER FIVE

LANDERS

A lander is a robotic craft that lands on an object in space. The first probe to ever touch down on another planet was Russia's Venera 7. The probe crashed on Venus's surface on December 15, 1970. For 23 minutes, Venera 7 sent data back to Earth. Then it stopped working. It is still there today.

SPACE FACT:

When Cassini was launched in 1997, Europe's Huygens lander hitched a ride. Huygens landed on Titan, one of Saturn's moons.

A Failed Mission

In 2015 the European Space Agency sent its lander Philae to study a comet. But Philae didn't land on the correct spot on the comet. Scientists lost its signal. Eventually, Philae was found when another probe took a photo of it. Philae had stopped working. It was stuck in a hole on the comet's surface.

In 2015 a model of the Venera 7 lander and parachute was displayed at The Science Museum in London, England.

NASA's latest lander touched down on Mars on November 26, 2018. InSight is equipped with instruments to measure temperature, wind, and even earthquake activity. InSight was accompanied by two miniature **satellites** called Mars Cube One, or MarCO. These satellites relayed information from the probe back to Earth.

SPACE FACT:

The MarCO satellites are nicknamed EVE and WALL-E, after characters in the 2008 Pixar movie *WALL-E*.

satellite—a spacecraft used to send signals and information from one place to another

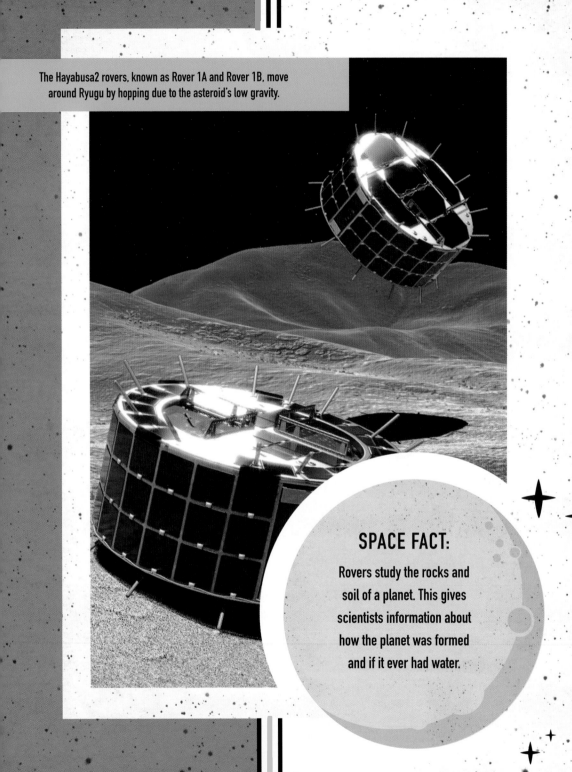

The Hayabusa2 rovers, known as Rover 1A and Rover 1B, move around Ryugu by hopping due to the asteroid's low gravity.

SPACE FACT:

Rovers study the rocks and soil of a planet. This gives scientists information about how the planet was formed and if it ever had water.

Landers can be used only once. After they land on the space object, there are no rockets to get them back to Earth. In 2014 the Japanese space agency JAXA launched a special probe called the Hayabusa2. This probe was designed to return after its mission.

In June 2018 the Hayabusa2 reached an asteroid called Ryugu. Hayabusa2 has four rovers onboard. Rovers are landers that explore, or rove, a planet's surface. Three of the rovers are on Ryugu, collecting information. The last one is scheduled to land in 2019. In time, Hayabusa2 will create a crater on Ryugu. Then it will collect the loose rocks and dust. At the end of its mission, Hayabusa2's reentry capsule will return to Earth with samples from Ryugu.

NASA launched two robot rovers called Spirit and Opportunity in 2003. They landed on different parts of Mars. This way scientists could study as much of the planet as possible. Their mission was to look for water. Humans need water to survive. If Mars has water, maybe humans could live there one day.

Spirit and Opportunity took a lot of colorful photos of Mars. Scientists discovered that Mars may have had water a long time ago. But it doesn't anymore.

Curiosity is another NASA Mars rover. Launched in 2011, it is collecting rocks and filming the planet's dust storms.

These Mars rovers are not designed to return to Earth on their own. But perhaps someday in the near future, astronauts will be able to walk on Mars and bring these rovers home.

SPACE FACT:

The Opportunity rover's mission ended on February 13, 2019. It was the longest-serving rover in NASA history.

CHAPTER SIX

WHAT'S NEXT?

NASA launched the Voyager 1 and Voyager 2 probes in 1977. Their mission was to fly by the outer planets of our solar system—Jupiter, Saturn, Uranus, and Neptune. They took pictures of these planets and their moons. No one on Earth had ever seen pictures like these. Soon after, the cameras on the Voyager probes were turned off to save energy. But some instruments are still working.

SPACE FACT:

The Voyager probes are carrying messages from Earth. If the probes come across other life-forms in space, these recordings could tell them about us and our planet.

The Voyager 2 is about the size of a dairy cow.

In 2012 Voyager 1 became the first human-made object to fly into **interstellar** space. This is the part of space that is beyond our sun's magnetic field. Voyager 2 crossed into interstellar space in November 2018. Scientists are now learning more about space just beyond our solar system.

These probes have been in space for more than 40 years. They will keep going until their power runs out. Who knows what else they will find out there.

interstellar—between stars, most often used to describe travel from one star to another

ICON will study the ionosphere about 350 miles (563 km) above Earth.

Countries around the world will continue to launch probes into space. European and Russian space agencies are working together to send the ExoMars rover to Mars in 2020. This lander's mission will be to look for signs of life on the planet. It will carry a drill to collect rock and mineral samples and return them to scientists on Earth.

India's Chandrayaan 2 probe will be heading to the moon in 2019. This probe has a lander, rover, and an orbiter. Once Chandrayaan 2 reaches the moon, the lander and rover will separate from the orbiter and land on the moon's surface. Then the rover will explore the moon.

Soon NASA will launch the Ionospheric Connection Explorer (ICON). It will orbit Earth and study the **ionosphere**. This will help scientists protect communication systems and technology in space. They will also learn more about this section of Earth's atmosphere.

Whatever their mission, space probes can do what humans can't. They can travel great distances and spend years in space. The information they gather will be useful for future space programs. Someday humans may even live on other planets because of the information learned from probes.

ionosphere—a layer of Earth's atmosphere; the ionosphere is 50 to 600 miles (80 to 966 km) above Earth's surface

GLOSSARY

asteroid (AS-tuh-royd)—a chunk of rock that orbits the sun; asteroids are too small to be called planets

atmosphere (AT-muh-sfeer)—the layer of gases that surrounds some planets, dwarf planets, and moons

black hole (BLAK HOHL)—an area of space with such a strong gravitational field that not even light can escape it

dwarf planet (DWAHRF PLA-nuht)—a space sphere that orbits the sun but has not cleared the orbit of neighboring planets

engineer (en-juh-NEER)—someone trained to design and build machines, vehicles, bridges, roads, and other structures

International Space Station (in-tur-NASH-uh-nuhl SPAYSS STAY-shuhn)—a place for astronauts to live and work in space

interstellar (IN-tur-stel-ahr)—between stars, most often used to describe travel from one star to another

ionosphere (EYE-uhn-oh-sfihr)—a layer of Earth's atmosphere; the ionosphere is 50 to 600 miles (80 to 966 km) above Earth's surface

orbit (OR-bit)—the path an object follows as it goes around the sun or a planet

satellite (SAT-uh-lite)—a spacecraft used to send signals and information from one place to another

solar flare (SOH-lur FLAYR)—gas that shoots out of the sun's surface

solar system (SOH-lurh SISS-tuhm)—the sun and all the planets, moons, comets, and smaller bodies orbiting it

READ MORE

Kortenkamp, Steve. *Mars Exploration Rovers: An Interactive Space Exploration Adventure.* You Choose: Space. North Mankato, MN: Capstone Press, 2017.

Riggs, Kate. *New Horizons.* Now That's Fast. Mankato, MN: Creative Education, 2018.

Siy, Alexandra. *Voyager's Greatest Hits: The Epic Trek to Interstellar Space.* Watertown, MA: Charlesbridge, 2017.

INTERNET SITES

Space Probes
https://starchild.gsfc.nasa.gov/docs/StarChild/space_level1/probes.html

NASA Jet Propulsion Laboratory
https://www.nasa.gov/centers/jpl/education/spaceprobe-20100225.html

INDEX